Amplified Silence

Dreamt I had drawn piano keys
on my kitchen table. I played on them, mute.
The neighbors came over to listen.

~ Thomas Tranströmer

Also by Kieran Egan

Tenure. Edmonton: NeWest Press, 2021.

Among the branches (Alfred Gustav Press) 2019

Learning in depth: A simple innovation that can transform schooling. Chicago: University of Chicago Press, 2011.

The future of education: Reimagining our schools from the ground up. New Haven: Yale University Press, 2008.

Building my Zen garden. Boston: Houghton Mifflin, 2000.

The Educated mind: How cognitive tools shape our understanding. Chicago: University of Chicago Press, 1997.

Teaching as story telling. Chicago: University of Chicago Press, 1989.

More books by Kieran Egan at:
   https://www.thriftbooks.com/a/kieran-egan/308780/

AMPLIFIED Silence

by

Kieran Egan

720 – Sixth Street, Box # 5
New Westminster, BC
V3C 3C5   CANADA

Title: Amplified Silence
Author: Kieran Egan
Cover Photo: "Crescent Beach Sunset" © Sharla Cuthbertson
Layout and Design: Candice James
Editor: Candice James

All rights reserved including the right to reproduce or translate this book or any portions thereof, in any form without the permission of the publisher. Except for the use of short passages for review purposes, no part of this book may be reproduced, in part or in whole, or transmitted in any form or by any means, electronically or mechanically, including photocopying, recording, or any information or storage retrieval system without prior permission in writing from the publisher or a licence from the Canadian Copyright Collective Agency (Access Copyright).

www.silverbowpublishing.com
© *Silver Bow Publishing 2021*
info@silverbowpublishing.com

isbn: 9781774031575 book
isbn: 9781774031582 e book

Library and Archives Canada Cataloguing in Publication

Title: Amplified silence / by Kieran Egan.
Names: Egan, Kieran, author.
Description: Poems.
Identifiers: Canadiana (print) 20210116285 | Canadiana (ebook) 2021011634X | ISBN 9781774031575
    (softcover) | ISBN 9781774031582 (EPUB)
Classification: LCC PS8609.G36 A76 2021 | DDC C811/.6—dc23

For Susanna,
always my first and best reader

Acknowledgements:

Many of these poems have been improved by the generous critical attention of my colleagues in the A-Drift Writers' Collective: Leanne Boschman, Adrienne Drobnies, Bill Ellis, Tom Gorman, Ken Klonsky, Christopher Levenson, and Nilofar Shidmehr.

Special thanks to Chris Levenson for patiently and skillfully mentoring a beginner in this business and reading and commenting on nearly all the poems in this book, and for his help in organizing the set of poems, and to Allan Briesmaster for help in editing and final shaping of this collection.

Some of these poems have been published in the following magazines: *Dream Catcher* (UK), *The Blue Nib* (Ireland), *English Bay Review* (Canada), *The Poetry Shed* (UK), *Plainsongs* (USA), *Sarasvati* (UK), *Dissonance (UK). The High Window* (UK), *Antigonish Review* (Canada), *Foxglove* (USA), *Dawntreader* (UK), *Grain* (Canada), *Canada Quarterly, Dalhousie Review* (Canada), *Galway Review* (Ireland), *Banyan Review* (USA), *Snapdragon* (USA), *Vallum* (Canada), *Acumen* (UK), *Literary Review of Canada, Event* (Canada*);* a few appeared in my chapbook *Among the Branches* (Alfred Gustave Press, Canada) and in the anthology *Old Bones and Battered Bookends,* Repartee Press, Canada. I am grateful to the editors for the hospitality of their pages, even though, on the Groucho Marx principle, I immediately wonder should I allow my poems to be published in a place that would accept them.

Contents

Unsettled

Happy Lightning ... 13
Sound Mind ... 14
Weakly Totter ... 15
Everyday Choices ... 16
Deserting Room... 17
Losing Touch ... 18
I Got the Dog ... 19
Night Noises ... 20
Death Faces Death ... 21
Bewitched in Dublin ... 23

Not the Best Journeys

Cultural Confusions ... 27
Burial Practices ... 28
Such A Journey ... 29
Not the Best Journey ... 31
An Old Captive ... 32
Required for Fighting ... 34
Alert to Landscape ... 35
Distracting Photos ... 36
On the Ferry ... 37
Expectations of Terror ... 38
Under an Eastern European Bridge ... 39
Crossing the River ... 40

On and Under the Ground

Close of Day ... 43
Under the Ground ... 44
Song of My Cabin Unroofed ... 45
The Tree at The Spring ... 46
Fall Ceremony ... 47
What Remembers the Children ... 48
Jaguar ... 49
Voices in Stone ... 50

Rising Among Branches ... 51
Playing a Cedar's Rings ... 52
Grasses of Kaliningrad ... 53
Winter Woodlands ... 54
Pine Needles ... 55
Getting Through Winter ... 56

Time and Change

The Past Reaches Forward ... 59
Slow Down, Lady ... 60
Ownership of My Body ... 61
Accumulating Shame ... 62
I'll Take You Home Again, Kathleen ... 63
Opportunities Lost or Unavailable ... 64
Slow Slaughter ... 65
Birthday Girl ... 66
Names Pass ... 67
Meeting History ... 68
Michael's Kite ... 69
Alien Ills ... 70
A Woman After My Own Heart ... 71
She Sits by the Sea ... 72

Galactic Hymns

Looking Inward from Margaret River ... 75
Flicker ... 76
Amplified Silence ... 77
An Engine in The Night ... 78
When the Moon Goes Away ... 79
Burn Whatever Will Burn   ... 81
The Lesser Mystery ... 82
The God's Presence ... 83
Compline's Embrace ... 85
No Sense of An Ending ... 86

Author Profile ... 87

Unsettled

Happy Lightning

Like a lightning flash that suddenly makes you happy,
like meeting that old man in a pub in the west of Ireland,
near the gray slabs of the Burren slicked with cold rain,
the pub's fire bright and warm
and he came over with a pint
chatting as though we were old friends.

And like kayaking
when the baby jelly-fish
pulsed by the million in the water beside us
as we moved among the islets of Masset Inlet,
climbing out onto treed half-acres
under clear blue sky,
the dark water shaded with green
from the forests around —
no human mark or stain was visible
except ourselves, resting on the paddles,
feeling blessed.

And like that young woman
above the cricket ground in Singapore,
both of us there by chance with no interest in the game
but pleased enough by the crack of bat against ball
and occasional shouts
while we discovered such pleasure
in one another's company.

Each felt like something miraculous
striking the ground around me,
as the mercy of god is supposed to change bleak lives.

And now, perhaps too late,
I pray for such a final flash
of sudden happiness.

Sound Mind

I was once of sound mind trailing a catcher's mitt
like a basket of multicolored hopes
at ease in the trees and fields on the edge of town;

I was once of sounder mind
sliding electric fingers tenderly down her naked arm
to rest in the nest of her welcoming hand;

doubts about my soundness of mind
emerging in shocked whispers
like hailstones skittering across the prairie,
marrying so young among my unready friends.

I might not have been of sound mind
buying the neglected farm,
our fluttering hearts' audacious gamble
as my wife for life hugged my anxious arm.

Soundness of mind still seemed at risk
wrestling stones, setting fence posts,
plant, cultivate, harvest with toughened hands,
the bedrock of new stock in the sagging old barn;

but who can remain of unsound mind
raising a flock of children,
like birds, wildlings on a reviving farm,
our nest blessed with their musical babel.

I no longer care if I am of sound mind,
leaning on my oak ridging-hoe,
hearing a thrush, a grandchild's laughter,
in a son's crisply furrowed field etched to the high woodlands.

Weakly Totter

Four arthritic knees, two stiff backs,
in a slow ambling ordeal down Main Street.
Entering shops, poking around, can't find anything to buy.
They stop for coffee to rest their pains.
Surprised, alarmed at growing old.

One mind formed from motorbikes, mountain climbing,
rowdy drinking, wildness still tousling his iron-gray head,
shadowed by dead friends.

The other, bald-headed, mind formed
in Benedictine monasteries
by plainchant, cloisters, ceremonies,
discipline held his hand and heart.

As they sat among the sounds of coffee making
and youngsters tapping at their screens,
the wild man said,
'Night has come over the Atlantic.
Can you see the chaotic mounds of thrashing water?'
It was a game they played each week.
'I can,' said the priestly friend. 'An all-directions storm,
deep-muscled waves slamming across each other,
like ancient soldiers fighting in the dark.'
'Ships are tossed about and swallowed in the deep.'
'Fish and whales, hunched in fear,
are thrown around like dead leaves in the wind.'
'And snow tumbles onto the towering surges.'
'Yes, I see snow falling into the dark ocean.'

Next door an antiques shop to pick through,
and after another half hour the tottering *flâneurs*
ambling to eternity down Main Street
will find a pub and pint to end the day.

Everyday Choices

You are preparing to turn right to your mother's
where we are expected soon for tea, but let's consider.
I have a credit card; you could drive on straight ahead
and within two hours we can catch a chunnel train,
then head south through France, a night in Paris,
another in La Rochelle, still reeking of history.

We'd inspect the occasional castle or chateau,
lunch with local wines by quiet roadsides,
dinners on balconies with trailing plants,
intimate moments between crisp French sheets.

Then we'd drive down the coast of Portugal
to Lisbon, where we might spend a day
and visit Jerónimos monastery again,
hand-in-hand along the wide double-decker cloisters,
ornately designed for the swagger of decadent abbots.

Then winding west along the coast road to Sintra,
taking an English tea above the glittering Tagus in Cascais,
imagining those ships heading out on the wind
to find new worlds.
In Sintra we can take a shaded room
for days at Lawrence's hotel,
where—is it a recommendation? —
Lord Byron stayed years before.
Or would you rather turn right now to your mother's?

I thought so. I left some items out of the equation.

Losing Touch

As I grow older, dearest one,
my life in this place
grows more insubstantial,
and the lives of others
in other times and places
grow vivid and more ample.

If this continues
I'll lose all contact
with this garden and this house,
find myself wandering
among foreign hills,
adrift through the streets of Asian cities,
my goat hooves clicking on craggy mountains,
licking my paws in a Brazilian forest.

Deserting Room

A room passes overhead,
without its furniture, ceiling, walls, and floor,
and the people;
just the space itself.

It catches in branches in the park
and settles there,
till children playing recognize it
and the dog who knows it well
barks and barks up into the tree.

At night, when the dog is dragged away
and parents tell insistent children to talk sense,
you can hear the murmur of voices from the room.

The essence of old contentment and old arguments
slides, dribbles into the grass.

When the family gathers among their walls and furniture
they know something is missing,
but they can't recognize what has left them,
nor how they might get it back.

I Got the Dog

I got the flea-tormented dog, brown matted fur and smell,
and the sorrier job of burying its master, my friend.
I swung the mattock to clear the last foot of clay —
ochre, blotched with olive, hard and knotty,
unyielding to the spade.
It may be a damp final house,
but he never minded being wet to the bone.

A curtain of black rain hisses across the corn,
sends ahead a shudder of wind.

Standing on the base of his eternal house
I find climbing out a struggle,
even helped by the hands of my dead friend's father.
Worse for him as the coffin is quickly lowered.
Then the smash of rain, and the soil, clay first,
is shoveled clattering down.
At the foot, his father wanted — 'an old man's fancy'—
a rowan tree, something to do with
singing to my friend when he was small.
Time now for us to scatter.

Neither its mother nor nature made the dog
an effective hunter of fleas in matted fur,
doing more damage to itself than to its tormentors.
In the rattling cart on the road that will become familiar,
the dog, tied in the back, bewildered, tried a whine.
Unprepared also for his first bath in a year.

Not an early death, like boys cut down in battle,
yet too soon, too much still to see and say and hold.
Perhaps it will comfort the dog and me to sit
where they so often sat together
looking over the corn field, even in rain.

Night Noises

Awake to creaking on the stairs —
by teenagers returning home, too late,
too early for mother-in-law's dawn tea.

The woken mind separates
the tentative feet of starting rain
across the roof from the scritching of racoons or rats,
and from the rain's confederate winds
straining the wood-framed house.

As the rain gathers strength, he is sad:
the teenagers are now long gone,
the mother-in-law is under the ground.

The years crowd together one on the next —
a short story he could crumple in his hand.

He creaks down the stairs,
trying not to wake his wife
or the visiting grandchildren,
to make his dawn tea,
to watch from his chair
the rain fall into the trees,
among the flowers, onto the lawn.

Death Faces Death

It used to be so easy culling us —
unclean, ill-fed, worn out, broken, leaking,
we were done by forty —
exhausted, we lay down and faced the wall.

After years of better food and sanitation
we still begin to crumble
before three score and ten.

But now the doctors fight for every extra month:
blocked arteries that used to finish us
are stented in an easy operation,
next day we're skipping grinning down the street;
failing organs get whipped out,
better ones slipped in;
ineluctable old killers now are harmless —
therapied, stem-celled, vaccinated, drugged.
Soon half the population
will be in their second century
running marathons.

'But you remain,' Death smiles,
'slaves to fate, chance, desperate men;
poison, war, and sickness still remain my allies.
Despite your desperate defences,
they will in the end defeat you.'

But soon, Death, very soon,
a few tweaked genes in embryos
will ensure for our descendants
that after twenty-seven years of growth
a full regeneration will kick in:
their bodies will remain forever young.

You scoff? You imagine problems
with this brave new world?

But who, in such a prime, will vote to die,
even after a thousand years or more?

Ask not for whom the bell tolls, poor old Death.

Our grandchildren's children will calculate
in centuries, millennia, even eons —
the new expensive rags of their extended time.

'Hard not to feel some sympathy
for those of you kicked off the stage just now,
the last to exit life the customary way,
bitter, resentful, leaving not a rack behind.

Come, hold arthritic hands with Death
and let us fall together into our long night
while others live their long, long day.'

Bewitched in Dublin

Late afternoon shadows in a silent room,
once elegant, and still so, though dust and time
now hang sluggish in the tired air
and small tatters on the velvet curtains
are new since the days I was at home here.
I stand and slowly walk its length and width,
then sit again in the green high-backed chair,
leather more stained and crackled than before.
From the first moment, my favourite room
I thought without thinking — she made it so.

When first we met after running into
Bewley's from a sodding autumn deluge,
both protecting copies of the same book,
we'd laughed and argued, and been surprised.
Charm, warm smile, yet distracted by something,
looking bleakly out the window.
She was an actress, she told me,
a haunting part which suited her because
'I'm maybe an ironic Irish witch.'

When rehearsing comic or tragic roles,
playing piano, even when angry,
always in her eyes the ghost of a smile.
She trod an outer edge of irony,
close enough to hold hands with mild madness —
witch or no, she bewitched.
She introduced me to her friends in pubs,
parties, 'This is my man who knows about hearts —
but only their plumbing,' with a wry shrug.

Invited to a Texas hospital
to learn new techniques of valve replacement —
'Come with me, I'm your heart man, after all.'

She said that I would cease to exist if I left.
She'd been true to her word —
not one word more did I receive —
emails and letters ignored, phone disconnected.

I'm back, half a dozen years behind us.
The flat is now for sale.
I sit in the green high-backed leather chair
and look around the lifeless room — wondering
would the witch come back and make it live again?

Not the Best Journeys

Cultural Confusions

A deserted diner off the highway;
watched by the dark-haired, heavy waitress
I ate alone and uncomfortable.
Something wrong with her right eye
so craning round to see me better with the left.
Her Wyoming vowels offered pie Alamo-ed,
or so it sounded to my English ear.
After we sorted that out she returned to lean and watch.
The coffee I ordered she placed down hard,
bending over me to ask, "Do you scream?"

Somewhere behind my ears splayed images
of weary torturers in Russian cellars,
racks, blades, Vlad, and Torquemada.
But here chainsaws for American carnage
in some slaughterhouse behind the kitchen.
Fight or flight, in turmoil to evade her half-closed eye.
Awareness seeping through my rising panic
of a small jug by my cup and
hearing the Wyoming, 'Do you use cream?'

The sagebrush grasslands outside the window
have known more brutal cultural confusion.
I can see red hills in the distance,
the scratched line of a road, some cultivated land,
other scars that might be fences,
where Red Cloud had imagined it
stretching unboundaried forever.

Burial Practices

The men were buried in thin coffins, upright,
ready to rage out and fight beside their kin,
bronze swords and daggers near skeleton fingers.
The women, expecting, at last, greater leisure,
lying splay-boned in the dust of what had been
reverently placed to equip their journey.
The graves set in a circle of ash trees,
and close to water — though rivers and flora
have changed from four thousand years ago.

Some carried the coffins that have long since rotted,
some said the equivalent of 'rest in peace',
some were broken hearted, some indifferent —
he meant more than the gods to one,
she left a hole in another's heart that was never filled —
and some delivered the sighs and groans
that death and burial always evoke.

The Hitachi back-hoe's steel teeth disinterred them
digging a nesting space for fuel tanks
in the motorway's new service station
The ready warriors sliced in half by the Hitachi's second bite,
their bones exposed, scattered in the soil;
the reclining ladies unscathed till archeologists arrived.

Not rising again as they had planned.
Useless at pumping petrol, changing tires,
and the ceaseless crowds that throng the forecourt
would lurch the heart of the bravest fighter.
The women's daily grind of cereal
would be confounded by the restaurant's food.
They would have gathered together,
at bay facing this altered world,
wary, bewildered, like the rest of us.

Such a Journey

Not the season we would have chosen for such a journey,
the fear of snow on the higher passes,
the car with its undiagnosed rattle,
and your arthritic parents complaining
of the cold, the hardship, the cost of those motels.

On the fourth day of the three we'd planned,
the snow locked us into a mountain village.
The motel staff hostile, the owners unfriendly,
the scummy garage across the street
could fix the rattle, smugly smiling, with,
for the price, a new timing belt made of gold.
Your parents sigh regrets at setting out,
folly to have come all this way, and now to be too late.

The next morning we risked an early start,
coming down to dry roads below the snow line
and made good speed racing
for some time beside a mile-long train
carrying god knows what to the interior.

The lakes with hardy boaters, kayakers,
bare vine rows waiting for summer sun,
meadows with black and white cattle,
a horse and foal cantering away from us.

There was still no phone reception, but we continued,
arriving at evening as the sun slid behind the mountains.
I parked, your parents tottered hastily
to greet the incarnation and epiphany of their new granddaughter,
held out to them by your exhausted and exalted sister.

The family is transformed;
each child brings a new dispensation.

We now go forward in the world
unknowably changed;
empowered, enlarged, enriched.

We returned to our homes
exhausted and exalted in our turn.

Not the Best Journey

The train to Warsaw stops among long Polish fields.
A wind from Germany scrapes all the trees
as far as Russia, annoying every branch and tired leaf
along a route taken often before,
and, hard to forget, sometimes in tanks.

The fields are prepared for winter once again —
each field a thousand years deep —
under a line of herons that have creaked overhead
at least as long.

Two mongrel dogs challenge the train
from the dirt road of their farm;
two dogs at home in this raw place.

An announcement of the reason for our delay
concludes, "We wish you the best journey."

From the window, mounded coils of razor wire
glitter below the farm's fence
beside tramped and littered grass,
to keep the aching feet of refugees
walking to the next country,
against the tank route,
trudging to Berlin.

An Old Captive

I share a Prophet and a God with Commander Ali
but it seems I am inadequately fervent,
so here I crouch, being spat on by a boy
who totes with easy assurance
a gun as big and frightening as himself
and waits to deliver casual death.

My house is now their house,
all decay and ruin,
valued only for its thick walls.
The boy squats on the windowsill
watching for a sign from his Commander.
A woman makes noises in the kitchen,
preparing food and pots of coffee.

I am torn by fear and bored by waiting,
not knowing what signal might come to the boy, nor when.
The woman walks in and out of the room
stirring the dust that coats the floor and rubble.
Some days the wind adds sand,
which settles in all corners of the battered building.
The house grows still and cold as the sun descends.
I grope for the sweaty blanket under remnants of my desk
while wolves call at night in the hills above.

My fervour on behalf of Prophet and God
was shown inadequate when I sent my son and daughter,
under cover of a stormy night, to the border
where my brother keeps them safe.
I cannot face another inquisition.

Escape for me is a hopeless hope —
the ruined town and hills to the border
a wilderness of guns and madmen.

In our dark room the boy must sometime sleep,
I have heard the gun barrel scrape upon the floor.
But I am stiff under my desk; I can move only slowly,
my eyes, nose, ears, no longer serve me well,
muscles weak strings, unsteady, I would stumble,
and the boy, whom nothing can get past,
will bring me down.

I know I'll not see my children again.

Required For Fighting

They took him likely because he was tallest,
though his walk had a kind of apology to it.
He returned four inches taller. The apology was replaced
by a style formed by daily carrying an AK-47.
Though his gentleness among the family goats remained,
something had gone wrong.
To one of the girls he said that he had been mostly
in the mountains, that in May the hillsides were covered
with purple flowers. Though he had been sent home,
he was waiting for something, and would leave again.

A Toyota truck came. He had a bag packed,
the AK-47 appeared from its hiding place.
He was ready. He did not say goodbye,
did not look at the goats or his family or the girl.

There was news of rebels, of a war, of brutal fighting.

He returned three inches taller, muscled, scarred.
He told the girl there were no flowers where he'd been,
among hills then hiding in a mangrove forest.

After three days we heard the clatter of an AK-47
during the night, and in the cool morning
found he had shot all the goats and then himself.

Alert to Landscape

He was fit into old age, my grandfather.
After driving out of the city each Sunday,
always in the latest big Mercedes,
he led the family walks
north into hills or east up the valley.
A tough face, serious and quiet,
his occasional smile lit up my world.

I noticed as I grew into my teens
he looked at the landscape
as though searching for something.
On our walks I observed, too,
a hint of urgency on valley floors.
Uneasy by the side of rivers,
he always led us toward more open ground,
his eyes alert to the hills and woods above.

I inherited the family photograph albums,
including one that had been kept from me.
Grandfather as a young man filled the first page,
commanding in the turret of a Panzer IV,
black leather jacket, Iron Cross at his throat,
advancing over a littered field near Kursk,
alert in that familiar way to the hills and woods around.

Reluctant inheritor of this suppressed
record of our family history,
I look again at the once loved face
under the peaked cap, with eagle and swastika.
In the album he is energetic, animated, happy,
as I had never seen him in my youth.
When I was young, he just seemed
what grandfathers were like.

(N.B. This poem is not autobiographical.)

Distracting Photos

Pensive, looking sideways, unfocused eyes,
perhaps wondering about her future.

Now flight-phobic, terrified of takeoffs.
To ease her anxieties I had suggested
we bring and talk about photographs of ourselves,
at ages five, and ten, fifteen, and twenty.

We examined the pensive ten-year-old girl looking sideways.
The woman she had become started to reminisce
about her family, her school,
and what the girl in the photograph most cared about.

It was just a few minutes' distraction,
neither of us foresaw the sobbing flood of tears.

On the Ferry

The small boy with the face of an intelligent angel
said solemnly, 'There are monsters at the bottom of the sea.'

'What kind of monsters?' his grandfather asked.
'They're coming for us,' the boy said.
'How can we stop them? Maybe the whales might eat them?'
'They are too powerful to be stopped.'
'What do they look like?'
'They're red-brown skeletons, with long curved horns;
they can bore holes straight up through this ship.'
'There must be some way to defend ourselves?'
'Nothing can stop them,' the boy said implacably.
'But skeletons need muscles to be able to move.'
'These skeletons can move.'
'Well, there must be something we can do?'

The boy said, 'It is hopeless.'

When the ferry carried them unmolested to the terminal
the boy sat unimpressed.

Expectations of Terror

There was no shelling
around the soccer field tonight,
no mortar attack
on the changing rooms,
no sign of tanks
on 41st. or MacKenzie.

The boys and their parents
took no precautions against sniper fire.
The helicopter not a gunship
but reporting on traffic for commuters.
No one ran for cover from that jet:
it was carrying executives to a meeting.
The bag the team mother carried
was packed not with grenades but oranges.
The families walked past lines of cars,
expecting none of them to explode.

Our houses have suffered
no destruction from bombs.
Our cats and dogs
have not gone mad or starved or been eaten.
If the kids win or lose this evening,
the wall will not detonate over them.

We are disturbed by
unfulfilled expectations of terror,
which is not the problem for others elsewhere.

Under an Eastern European Bridge

In a foul sleeping bag under the bridge,
mouse-coloured rags, mouse-coloured hair,
and her liver contributing mouse-coloured skin,
she sees the moon rising on the rising river.

Her tattered, defeated night-companions
have all deserted, departed.

The night is cold, the dark water colder,
as well to let it come, take her away.

Or scuttle out, getting her ankles wet.
And tomorrow beg food again, find another bridge?

She has a pencil, picked up outside the post-office,
and a torn piece of discarded packing paper,
thinking to tell the story of what brought her here
from the family villa outside Poznan.

She started: 'I had a happy childhood,'
and ended one line later,
'and so I can survive almost anything.'

Crossing the River

Charon's boat was full — I could wait on his return —
"You're in no hurry!" he laughed, pushing away into the mist.

"Alternatively . . ." a smiling ruffian in a creaky coracle
offered his ferry service. Shrugging, I gave him my obol.

Inexpertly he took us into a current that swept us far downstream,
well beyond the land of the dead, beyond any land I'd heard of.

Emerging from the mist we saw by the river's rocky edge
crowds of handsome people watching us incuriously.

"These are the unborn," he said, "who were due to join the living,
but something intervened so here they wait, I know not for what.

"Maybe some, maybe many had an intimation
of what lay ahead for them and chose to remain unborn.

"On this shore they're at their ideal age, peak of health and vigor,
they are unnamed, unmemoried, unminded,
but beautiful, unspoiled by life.

"This is a land of waking sleep,
dreamless for them so not quite sleep,
immortality broods over them, yet
they remain untroubled in their silence.

"I mostly envy them and feel they daily have
what I toiled for all my life and failed to find.

"We could disembark here if you wish,
or I could struggle back upriver to Hades,
where I'm also due myself."

On and Under the Ground

Close of Day

Dusk on a gray day
crows have already filled
the trees around the lake

the wind rises
carrying woodsmoke
ruffling tail feathers
and makes the water shiver

clouds so high
they do not seem to move

two lovers walk apart among the trees

a mournful tune whistled
by a boy in a canoe

there's a background hum
from cars along the highway

green shadows blacken

great wings easing it down
a solitary heron
returns late home.

Under the Ground

To creatures with coarse ears,
gardens grow in silence.
Finer instruments hear the creak,
the strain, the groaning urge,
the boulder crash of soil
brutally pushed aside.
Each stem screeching upward,
flowers thundering into air,
exploding into colour.

The finest filaments of roots
sucking like a million pigs
beneath your lawn
slurping at the flood of rain.

And we are deaf to the
eruptions of trees' roots
smashing all in their way,
of massed armies
of screaming grubs
fighting for life and food,
eating and being eaten,
uncountable losses and gains
in relentless offensives.

That they are so small is nothing.

Song of My Cabin Unroofed by Spring Fire

Acknowledgements to Du Fu: 茅屋為秋風所破歌:
"Song of My Cottage Unroofed by Autumn Gales"

I lie among bluebells in the woods behind the cabin,
coughing, smudged, and sick
from brawling with the smoke and fire
that have destroyed what my father built.

The day is ending with the sour smell of wet ash,
with the touch of flames on my lips and hands.
The cabin is gone, despair and family history
leak away with the last trailing smoke.

Perhaps it was always too cold in winter,
lately too small for our growing family,
insecure against thugs, thefts, and damage.

I lie among the bluebells thinking
of our children's futures,
like far-away countries,
and separated by this further grief.

If only I could build a sturdy house
of a thousand, ten thousand rooms,
enduring as a mountain of strong stone,
to fill with all my family and friends
and keep them close — a sigh —
where we could live a thousand, ten thousand years,
though in such a joyful place
ten days, even one day would be enough for me,
if they could ever after be secure.

The Tree at the Spring

This crooked tree by the stream's side
groans with the effort of new leaves emerging
and with the tawdry load its branches bear:
ribbons, beads, a pair of baby's shoes,
plastic-wrapped messages and prayers and verses
for children lost or in danger —
branch by branch, heartbreak upon heartbreak.

Our own children's radiant faces come to me;
my exaltation always tied to a deep fear
that has not diminished since the day each was born,
and which no holy spring or tree or prayer can ease.

Fall Ceremony

A late October afternoon
a woman and nine or ten year old son
engage in the ritual
of raking amber, red, and browning leaves,
discovering again their neat green lawn
as the boy pushes with gloved hand
the last clump onto the rake
and carefully lifts it towards
the open bag his mother holds.

But a bent tine catches the bag's lip,
scattering the leaves back onto the grass.

They groan, then laugh together
as he bends to scoop them up again.

This moment
       will be, for one,
     paradise lost;
          for the other,
         paradise now.

What Remembers the Children?

In winter the garden's tired grass does not recall
the children's summer games,
nor does the cherry tree —
bright blossom, black fruit —
remember the stories they told in its branches.

Their years of laughter and shouted quarrels
are not recorded in the cedar's rings,
and the dog barks into the air next door
the same response to any movement
as to their forgotten games of tag.

The goldfish, all instinct, no memory,
take food as readily from others
as from the children who gave each a name.

It is proper for everything in nature to forget,
except for the root of this writing hand.

Jaguar

She knows I am no threat to her, and she has recently eaten,
long-dead meat she had not herself brought down,
and there is a heavy chain-link fence between us.
I look at her patterned gold-brown body
resting in the grass, preferring sleep in the sun
no doubt, to this edge of wariness
my idle presence keeps her in.
No threat, but why am I still here? —
we both wonder.

After some minutes she opens gold eyes, slowly,
and looks ahead, not deigning to turn their glory
towards me, though I can feel her attention.
She eases out a deep low rumble
that makes my stomach tighten.
Alert for a wrong movement,
narrowing the kohl-black eyelids
that said next will be claws, then teeth
and a lunge towards your throat
faster than you can imagine.

What happened to her lowland forest?
The sharp sting of the dart,
and waking in this northern zoo.
Does she notice the different stars?

A nocturnal hunter, pushed into the noonday sun.

I want to treat her as a guest, to offer something —
though I can think of nothing she would value
apart from this body I'd rather keep intact —
something to expiate guilt
for our treatment of the wild things of the earth.

Voices in Stone

Three kangaroo families
among a copse of gum trees at mid-day
casually watch us trek toward the hills
through wide undulating rising land
and scattered stones.

Others listened for ancestral voices
in the slow wind where we rise among the rocks.

We climb to see swirling patterns
carved in boulders —
preserved shapes of those voices
dreaming in the depths of time.

When the wind drops,
in the vast air silence,
enough to swallow everything we know.

Swirls and lines and waving patterns,
etched by those who lived and died here long ago,
tell of trails to water, food, and shelter,
which we, banally, carry in our back-packs.

We return in silence,
feet padding unfamiliar soil and scrub,
with a kind of fear:
the weariness and wariness of trespassers
on land which is, to others, who they are.

Rising Among Branches

He had always been a great climber of trees.
A part of his wife's 'better or worse' promise
had formed itself unexpectedly into settled fear
that one day, one day . . .
or, later, merciful god, the limbs, the crack,
the broken body might be one of the children's.

But he had learned how to place each foot
on which branch in which weather,
and the patience came with him somehow.

So each child was carefully schooled
in joining the trees in rising from the earth.
No falls, no cracked heads, no bandaged limbs.

They developed, like him,
distance in their eyes.
And he took each grandchild
in turn
among the branches.

They all became friends with trees,
seeing them almost
like members of the family.

Playing a Cedar's Rings

You can count back your years in wavering rings
on the cross-cut end of a beached cedar.

From the bark inward
no more than a thumb's length
of a stump as big as you, marks off your life.

As your finger glides slowly round each ring
you release memories of green summers
and the songs of long-dead birds.

Children stop and listen
all the way down to the sea,
elders remember long-ago walking in woodland.

The tree unfolds,
cracking, brokenhearted,
leaves, insects,
wind and rain,
singing birds.

Grasses of Kaliningrad

The colored grasses of Kaliningrad,
are high as a boar's head or a wolf's ear.
There's a million densely crowded acres
that boar and wolf can hardly penetrate.
Russets, whites, yellows, and tall poppy heads.
Rushes, sedge and fragrant fennel thicken
where lines of dark green shrubs mark hidden streams.

All grass is flesh; these grasses thrive on flesh,
and their dense vigor shows they feasted well
on days dead men were scattered by the ton.
Rooted now round soldiers' bones, through field-grey rags
and rotting boots, corroded guns and shells,
in windy nights the grasses moan in German.

Winter Woodlands

Something glimmers in the winter wood,
metal, wet, or bird's eye.

Something coloured in the gray light,
berries, moth, or blue fly.

Something echoes through the branches,
wood-crack, rain, or vole's cry
as the vole and the owl come together
and the broken branch with the saffron wound
is brought softly to ground by frost and snow.

I turn towards home, to tea, book, curtains, lights,
under day's pale moon, half the size of night's.

Pine Needles

Picking pine needles gently out of moss,
thumb and forefinger sliding in to pinch,
to lift, to flick into the compost bag.

When too many fall from wind-rattled branches,
they bind into a mat that kills the moss,
aided by the murky pee of racoons,
or skunks, rats —I never catch them at it.

The incurious koi observe my sitting by the hour.

But soon I'll need to up and work for them
cleaning the pond's pump, taking the filter apart,
fingers in to swish out clogging needles.

It's not James Bond work,
not a roulette table and svelte woman
dark-eying me across the casino
in the capital of Exotica.

But after a pacific hour or two,
an immaculate patch of damp moss
green as God,
quiet as my heart.

Getting Through Winter

Showered, jet-lagged,
reluctantly prepared for work,
I stand at a hotel window after dawn,
dazed by snow and ice to the horizon.
Two ragged columns of smoke hang
like decomposing angels in the frigid air.

Railway tracks and bridges, steel tight with cold,
curve around and span a frozen river.

In last night's over-heated restaurant
the locals boasted to stunned, then wilting, visitors
about the toughness of the wildlife here:
the chickadees surviving minus thirty
and forty mile an hour ball-wincing winds,
and tree frogs that freeze until their hearts stop,
then wait for spring to kick them back to life.

Below, my colleague in the parking lot,
black-suited, garment bag over one arm
brief-case, keys, and high-heels gathered in the other,
walking stiff-legged towards her car.

I too must get down into the metal-bound throng
and drive past woods with hidden chickadees
and tree frogs whose frozen hearts wait, wait for
the north to lean towards the sun.

Time and Change

The Past Reaches Forward

Looking at the house where he'd once lived —
confidently standing four-square still —
somehow makes what has happened since
seem less substantial.

His real life, the old house asserts,
was what had happened here,
with the children on the swing,
laughter round the table, TV movie nights,
her flower garden, his vegetables,
the daily rush of noisy life.

However vivid, however happy
his present life, its better house,
its new and cheerful children,
he cannot suppress resentment
of the life his new love lived before they met
and fears that she must feel the same.

Does her remembrance of her past
drain substance from their present,
as it seems inexorably to do for him?

Do the colours of her life now
seem less bright
than remembered colours then?

And is this love inescapably second-hand,
comparatively worn and tired,
as the past reaches forward
with its claim of greater authenticity?

Slow Down, Lady

Slow down, lady, slow down.
It's not pockets full of lead,
but knees without cartilage,
lungs with fibrosis,
and too many years
in which time has battered the rest of me.

I stop, can't keep up with you,
watch you big-stride away
along the busy sidewalk.

Twenty seconds before you realize
you're not still dragging me
in your whirling wake.

'What's wrong?' you call.
"Knees, lungs, time."

People look from you to me,
making what they can or will of it:

it is just the born-work-die routine;
you're vigourously working,
I'm resting between gigs.

Ownership of My Body

My doctor owns my body,
reluctantly he lets me take it home with me,
knowing I'll pour alcohol into it,
eat too much meat, too little fruit and veg,
have cookies with my coffee,
and sit it down for extended hours in chairs.

His chronicle of my life-long abuse
is stored on his computer.
X-rays, blood tests, injuries, surgeries,
reports from specialists:
a multi-megabyte litany of abuse,
damage, and decay.

My caring doctor is due to retire,
and his admonitions grow more urgent:
'At seventy,' he says, 'the gun goes off —
your crumbling organs race to see
which one can kill you first.'

I'm an unreliable subaltern
in his struggle to keep my body functioning.

He fears that, lacking his dutiful care,
some new doctor will examine me
as might a casual statistician,
idly calculating how soon
    to archive my file.

Accumulating Shame

He would be ashamed of me now,
would not easily forgive me.
How could I face him
after all the ways I have let him down?

He had prepared this body well,
muscled, flexible, able for anything,
and look at it now . . . or, better, don't —
the firm and gleaming sheen his youth had honed
some vandal has despoiled
and left me with this sour and shabby wreck.

All that reading he did,
Russian novels, French literary theory,
irregular verbs of foreign languages,
names, dates, events from the beginning
of our species to yesterday's papers —
all virtuous, valuable knowledge,
now sieved away as my brain shakes
this way and that while looking for entertainment.

His exercise of self-control, his disciplines,
care for truth, cure for souls,
his meditations on how best to live —
some villain gradually traded them
for comforts, easier satisfactions.

Which of his enemies brought me to this?

"I'll Take You Home Again, Kathleen."

My Tipperary grandfather sang it constantly, mournfully.
His wife was called Bridget.
Twenty years in the British army in India,
and maybe fields fresh and green were
as important to his exile heart as any Kathleen.

His stories — playing cricket at Maharaja's palaces,
caparisoned elephants, peacocks, eager servants,
and summers in the paradise of Simla.

The Irish Bridget was forty when he married her.
They quarreled through fifteen years of my youth,
as he crouched by the coal fire trying to get India-warm again.

After another fight— "Not in front of the boy!" she'd shout —
he'd give me sixpence to buy sweets.
I'd sometimes return to him sitting alone,
damp handkerchief shielding tears.

In the glowing embers perhaps he'd seen old landscapes
and the dark beauty, Kaarina, Kavita, Kelila, Kumari,
whom, with much regret, he had not taken home
to his fresh green Irish fields.

Unsure by then where home was
and why she wasn't part of it,
imagining Kaarina there
and Bridget not.

Opportunities Lost or Unavailable

What choices had she made, what mistakes,
that led to her sitting with a Mythos beer
looking down at this gleaming yacht —
easing into Hydra's horseshoe harbor —
at those people lolling with champagne
looking up at her, a tourist at a bar?

The man she married and the man she longed for
were not the same, and the latter fool
assumed the marriage vows he'd made
when he married her best friend were to be kept.
And the former fool she'd married and divorced
had left her barely comfortable.

A yacht and champagne might offer consolations
but the bikinied girls, trying to look languid as in ads,
were hardly older than her schoolgirl daughters.
She'd have to settle for the crowded ferry
back to Spetses, where dinner loomed
at her hotel with the usual bunch of bores.

She'd splurge some Euros for a horse and carriage ride
from harbor to hotel along the coastal road.
The grizzled driver would reach to a bougainvillea
and with practiced charm hand back a flower
for her to tiredly smile and slip above her ear,
which nobody she cared about would see.

Surely some women unsung by bards
got the right man and the yacht?

But, as it was, the fool she'd married and the fool she longed for
were cycling together round the west of Ireland;
resistant saint and dreary scholar happily pedaling away.

Slow Slaughter

In old age the accumulating hurts
of removing socks, pulling on socks,
buttoning and un-buttoning shirts,
zipping and unzipping, un-belting and belting,
cleaning teeth, clipping nose-hairs,
is slow slaughter.

The tedium of boiling water,
making more damn tea,
finding a clean spoon,
is slow slaughter.

Breaking a shoelace, crying, sitting to pee,
squeezing toothpaste onto the razor
while knees, neck, back,
both feet and each thumb hurt,
is slow slaughter.

Between removing one sock and the next,
turning out the light.
Choosing to button, zip, and tie no more,
brush, polish, wash no more;
no triumphs wait ahead
no love or ease from pain,
just slow slaughter.

Old men are dry leaves drifting into soil,
dead whales drifting to the ocean floor.

Birthday Girl

At her fortieth birthday dinner,
her parents tell again their stories of her birth:
the swirling snow, the skidding car,
her mother's battle with the urge to push,
certain they'd not make it to the hospital in time.

The nurse wheeling her at speed along the corridor,
father climbing into gown and hat
for their rehearsed coaching of mother
through the waves of pain.

Hints of dark hair as the head emerged,
shouted encouragement from nurses,
and then the lovely girl,
arriving like a bullet that seemed, they smile,
to set her character for life.
Father holding her at dawn
as the sun's slow light slid down the snow-clad mountains.

When younger the birthday girl resented
their appropriating her great event,
but she had no competing memories.

Now she smiles indulgently;
already with a note of sadness: soon enough,
there will be no one who remembers.

And, soon enough, as adults, her grandchildren,
and certainly their children,
will not remember her birthday,

and, soon enough,
no one will know she'd been born.

Names Pass

Why does this man, approaching death,
work so hard to learn the names of plants,
or that one, heart stammering towards its cease,
struggle with Greek irregular verbs
to be able to read Thucydides before he dies,
or why does she sit with cancer
and telescope and night-sky charts
memorizing yet more stars and nebulae?

What use, what satisfaction to take into the dark
the accumulated names
that crumble into nothing at our death?

From the beginning the plants were indifferent
to being named by us; the stars have maybe
better names among inhabitants of closer planets,
and Thucydides' pleasure at being read
stopped at the moment of his own death.

And yet it seems heroic to enlarge our hoard,
to enjoy the power this knowledge gives us
a while longer, continuing with final urgency
to mark our brief dominion over all the earth we name.

Meeting History

'Today's a holiday,' my grandson said,
'it's Dr. Martin Luther King Jr. Day.'
He repurposed some more Lego blocks
from my medieval castle to enhance the
spaceport for his Millennium Falcon,
stacking yellow blocks into a look-out tower.
'I met Martin Luther King,' I told him.
He stopped dismantling my castle:
'How?' he asked. Not when or where.
As plausible to him as my meeting
Caesar, Napoleon, George Washington;
all equal parts of school's ghost world
in which jumbled bits are being assembled.

'In the Hilton Hotel, in London long ago,
when I was a student there.'
Vague and sharp in memory now:
the quiet voice, formidable presence.
'Forgive' and 'love' and 'hope,'
the themes of his gently rhythmic talk.
None of us prepared for the ramifying impact
of this serious man about serious business.
Hard now not to think also of Gandhi and Mandela,
each hoping for just a little better from the rest of us
while they shouldered the impossible,
not hesitating to move into the face of hate and horror.

'No, we weren't best buddies.
"Met" was a quick hello, a shake, and nod
as we left the room.'
My grandson stared, struggling to match this up
with lessons from the world of school;
a first spider thread beginning to tie
the ghostly past to his bright present.

Michael's Kite

Michael loosed his first kite
free to climb its first wind,
the spool spinning in his hands;
the dragon eagerly flapped into the sky
shaking its green head, fighting to escape
in sudden slanting dives and soars.

The string rose to a graceful bellied line,
and spun to the end of the roll
                                    which was not tied.
With a leap of raw joy the kite burst its tether —
out over the bay toward the city towers.

Father and son, we stood helpless,
eyes tied to the tricksy sprite
as it bucked and danced into the blustery heavens.
Michael distressed, thrilled, as it
rose higher than the highest skyscraper.

The dragon slowly diminished, fading
like the wind rush of days
into our insufficient memories.

Alien Ills

We hear of ways the body goes awry
from TV shows, the papers, or we're told
the alien ills one's friends succumb to:
hemoglobin balances in riot,
gridlocked endocrinal glands and colons.

Who knew our hearts go wrong so many ways?
Too fast or slow or leaking here or there,
or, worse, just stopping in the street one day.

Deranged cancers are the star performers,
that muck up any organ's functioning.
Auto-immune should be against the rules:
whose side's your body meant to battle for?
Simple basic workers, breasts or prostates,
maliciously betray you without cause.

Hearing friends recite these grotesque stories,
one's face puts on that strain around the eyes,
mouth solemn with attentive sympathy.
And then one has to add a further wince:
the awful side-effects of potent drugs
restricting life, to gain a little more.

But now these ills are suddenly one's own,
which, first, is surely some absurd mistake.
Then one makes adjustments to the error:
the pills, the slow recoveries from ops,
statistician doctors' admonitions,
the exercises, deprivation, pain,
displace the proper regulation of one's life.
We daily spend more effort on the body.
There's new routines and tricks one has to learn,
and it gives less, then much less, in return.

A Woman After My Own Heart
for Dr. Jacqueline Saw

She was in the driver's seat when I arrived,
calm, cool despite the sense of urgency.
Unfamiliarly drugged, I left her to it.

Slicing down the slip road,
accelerating into the arterial highway,
her raucous rock favorites cranked up high,
she was quickly pushing forward; I could feel it.
Blurred, hazy I tried to follow on the live navigation map.
Dark, wet, wreckage ahead, but I was in her hands now.

'Not my taste', I mumbled about the music,
but no one paid attention.
I could feel the speed as she threaded through tight passes,
discomfort — maybe she was taking the curves too fast,
but I let the drugs push all that away, relax.

We reached the place earlier than I'd expected,
maybe I'd slept some of the way.

'She's such a perfectionist,' said the nurse beside me.

Then she was flirting around with my heart,
a brief affair, just a tease, withdrawing,
leaving her stents behind.

Still, my heart flooded with gratitude.

She Sits by the Sea

Gray hair, thin now but still some curl,
she sits on a bench by the sea
looking across to the mountains.
Winter coat, a silk scarf against the autumn chill.
The name of the town
whose high-rises she looks at to her right
                      she cannot recall.
Nor — she is suddenly anxious —
how she got here. Someone surely
                      brought her in a car
and — she tries to convince herself
after looking around —
                      would also take her back —
back to   where her room is.
Some people walk by on the beach.
Two handsome men come towards her, smiling,
calling her by her name.
No, not her name — that's not her name!
Each takes an arm; they walk her to a car.
They know her, all is well.
They call her Mom.

Galactic Hymns

Looking Inward from Margaret River

Driving from Perth south to Margaret River,
late in a warm and velvet evening my friend pulled off the road
onto a dirt track where we bumped and swayed.
A fenced-off field on one side, rows of vines on the other.
I turned to ask where we were going.
    'Wait' he said.

Slowly onward some minutes more.
slow rocking in the dim glow from a moonless sky.
He cut the engine.
    'Wait.'

We sat in silence, the vine rows black on dark.
    'We can get out now.'

Electric insect noises, horses snuffling nearby, smell of manure.
    'Look up,' he said.

A smear of muted colours spread across the sky
bright, clear, benumbing, our Milky Way
as this city boy had never seen it.

From the viewing platform of our remote planet,
a billion stars spread out below me.

    'The centre of our galaxy is there,' he pointed,
        his finger tip blacked out
            stars, nebulae, galaxies.
He seemed to know his way around.

I looked inward at that blurred and bulging glow,
for a moment fearing I might stumble,
fall forward down into that central light
and further down into the Black Hole at its heart.

Flicker

In a dark field
a winter bonfire
crackles sparks into the sky;
our cosmic bonfire vents
a scatter of reeling galaxies
flickering on, flickering out.

The seeming succession of minutes, millennia,
the four-billion years of Brahma's Kalpa cycle,
cycles and epicycles,
whose spokes zip by in a zettasecond,
     every thirty trillion years,
          flicker,
               flicker.

Sometimes it feels our Kalpa is barely underway:
we're in the first flash of a zettasecond;
in a mere millennium there will be megacities
on megaplanets in megagalaxies.

Sometimes, near the end:
galaxies flailing apart at unimaginable speed,
the most distant invisible,
unknowable to ours, as ours to them.

We are particles of something
that can neither know itself or be known;
each of us a floating coral
fixing to its random necropolis;
billions of years past, billions to come
only this thin moment infected by us;
ash from our bonfire
invisible on the dark ground.

Amplified Silence

When the music stops my old speakers emit a slight hum
that sounds like distant cicadas or the faintest hiss of tinnitus.

Recently a girlfriend said,
as we sat after a song had ended,
'How quiet your room is.'
We listened —
I to the speakers' hum, she to silence.
What would she hear, that silence switched off?

All our sounds leave diminishing traces
that fade into the air around us.
The song, her words about the quiet room,
ebb and are lost, drifting into faintest stirrings
in the atmosphere, rearranging atoms somewhere.
But one day soon we will discover
how to hear those sounds again,
sucking them from the sky by some
unimaginable technology —
like DNA to former generations
or the X-Rays we now take for granted.
We will locate, capture, interpret and replay those traces.

Our children or their children will download the app,
alert the enhancers probing the atmosphere,
tune their amplifying Voice-Finder's
infinitely sensitive electronic ears
and be able to listen to every word ever spoken.

Tune in Cleopatra meeting Caesar,
Shakespeare chatting in a pub,
Eloise whispering to Abelard,
draft of a poem read by Du Fu,
your mother talking to you in childhood.

An Engine in the Night

I hear an engine working in the night,
its thrum distant, unfamiliar,
now amplified now fading on the wind.

Beyond Arbutus St., the ice rink perhaps?
Or further and higher, the pumping station
that drives the water to the reservoir?
An idling refrigerated truck delivering meat?
Mopeds racing through the park?

Apocalyptic horses cantering in line?
Or over the horizon, driving the axle of the earth?
Beyond the escarpment, a roaring machine,
big as the devil, tearing out houses by their roots,
scything lamp posts and fences, grinding up cars, buses, roads?

I part the curtains
and see the streetlights' glow against the clouds;
the sound comes from everywhere I look.
I return to bed uneasy
as the thrum subsides,
afraid of what will happen if it stops.

When the Moon Goes Away

Some love the sound of the ocean,
the tides rippling over pebbles,
the hiss of waves on sand,
the grating roar of breakers —
it's endless ebb and flow.

But one day soon the moon will move away
and the tides will come slowly to a standstill,
leaving a melancholy, long, withdrawing silence.
The sea will be calm tonight and every night:
those placid acres, that darkling plain's taut surface
whose leaden water hangs like mercury.

When the intrusive moon is gone —
inconstant, in the end faithless —
the wind and sea will be alone at last,
and we will become expert in the new shapes
into which wind moves tideless water.

Demosthenes long ago,
mouth full of stones,
would have faced no challenge from this turbid sea,
and into Sophocles' mind
the lack of ebb and flow
would bring again his certainty
that love alone can free us
from all the weight and pain of life,
dissolve the grief we cause ourselves
searching for absent waves on this featureless plain.

Ah, love, come
let us walk along the unchanging shore line.
The flat water looks as though its surface
could hold us up, if we had faith.

The black heads of seals poke through its membrane,
then return to their buried life, benumbed,
with the incurious fish.

Give me your hand.
Under moonless sky, by heavy waters,
we are no longer unsettled by restless sea.

Burn Whatever Will Burn

Taste the air, each breath a cough.
To the south, some say,
in hidden caves
you can breathe sweet air
cool as pearls.

Devotees of the God
of the Burning Forests
set fire to whatever remains
including their ecstatic selves,
screaming their anthem:

> *God the Fire,*
> *God the Sol,*
> *and God the Burning Ghost.*

The sky is dense with smoke, soot,
fried resins, sulfides, char, and ash.

I remember the night sky;
sharp stars, pale moon.
Day now is just less dark time,
sun a barely lighter patch
moving above us.

Apples burst into flame on the trees,
horses shriek leaking milk-white blood,
and the taste of fire is everywhere.

> *In the name of the Fire,*
> *and of the Sol,*
> *and of the Burning Ghost.*

The Lesser Mystery

The Scheduler of my dreams,
with sadistic glee, last night
programed applying for jobs
I have no hope of getting:
botched interviews, sweating fear, contempt;
as bad as my straining efforts to fly,
when I cannot pick up speed
and flail to rise above waist height,
while thrashing through snared corridors
that labyrinth for miles.

We give up the controls
as we pass through dreams' distorting mirror;
no negotiation, no truce within
our lesser mystery, little death.
Escaping sleep's dark grip
gives only desolate relief:
something precious has been stolen,
lanes and bridges ripped away
preventing passage back
to right the wrongs, to fix the problems
as we emerge from half-sleep
disinherited.

My Scheduler's preference for deranged nights
leads him with exquisite sadism
to occasionally interrupt regular programming,
and I awake some mornings radiant,
my sun-bright ships breasting the harbor.

The God's Presence

1

Milk and salt in ivory bowls
carried reverently
down the steps into the god's sanctuary,
and a drop of blood,
which you will contribute at the altar.
There is a warm mist, a stream nearby,
and pale fluttering shadows
behind the curtain of delicate muslin,
sibilant whispers around the columns
that sound like words
but not words you understand,
perfumed wafts of unfamiliar scents —
and that feather touch on your arm,
like an eyelash slowly
flickering towards your shoulder,
is the mark of the god's presence.

2

Too long ago, too far away,
you may be thinking,
from the new gods of Instagram and Twitter,
who require no sacrifice,
neither fasting nor penitential acts,
no ceremony or libations,
to access their holy places.
Stroke and tap, stroke and tap
on glass and plastic and you are among
their treasures in the cloud.
The unceremonious strokes and taps
do not bring us to the presence of the gods
but to clothing, games, kitchen appliances,

which algorithmically seek us out
though we think we are the seekers.
Do your gods dazzle or illuminate
or neither dazzle nor illuminate?
But you have to fear your gods
for their chrism to sanctify you.

3

The power of the techlords who tend
and service the new gods is great
but they neither instill fear
nor deliver a more sanctified self;
the techlords are omnipresent
but their gods elude us, have maybe left.
Their offer of salvation
seems unlike any form
we had been prepared to recognize.
We stroke and tap, stroke and tap,
distracted beneath the agitated cloud
by images and music of the living and the dead,
and sounds that sound like words
but scatter into excess of meanings
that call all in doubt.

The compasses no longer work
and sense and memory drain away,
''tis all in pieces, all coherence gone.'

Compline's Embrace

Be sober and vigilant: because your adversary the devil
goes around like a roaring lion seeking whom he may devour.
—The first epistle of St. Peter the Apostle: 5, 8.

Time and the devil,
our roaring adversaries,
are brought to slow silence
among the choir stalls.
Waves of plainchant
insistent as the sea
hold them in check.

Darkness nestles among the trees outside.
The friars have finished Compline and now kneel
among shadows and the crack of cooling oak.

Cowls up, they turn into the jaws of the choir stalls and pray,
clawed but undevoured by the lion day.

No Sense of an Ending

We are stories that set out one morning
And walk straight into wintery evening.
The end is upon us without warning.
Our world has turned yet we lack seasoning.
We rose and dressed, in lighted rooms took tea,
woke during anxious nights, stretched in the sun
on foreign beaches, watched the moving sea
in wonder, laughed with friends, left much undone.
At night we come to the departure dock.
Lights on the water, but there is no boat.
Strange silence after all the words and talk
and all the meanings that were too remote.
Ah, it comes to us and goes without warning.
We were short stories that set out one morning.

Author Profile

Kieran Egan lives in Vancouver, British Columbia, Canada. His chapbook, *'Among the branches'* was published by Alfred Gustav Press, in June, 2019. He was shortlisted for the Times Literary Supplement Mick Imlah prize in 2017 and the Acumen International Poetry Competition, 2020,

Kieran's poems have appeared or are forthcoming in the Canadian magazines Event, Quills, Literary Review of Canada, Dalhousie Review, Grain, Qwerty, Antigonish Review, Vallum, Canadian Quarterly, Ekphrastic Review, Spadina Literary Review, Pace, English Bay Review, Prairie Fire, and in the UK in High Window, Orbis, Envoi, Acumen, HQ Poetry Magazine, Interpreter's House, Dream Catcher, Dawntreader, Sarasvati, and The Poetry Shed, and in a number of U.S.A. magazines. His novel, *Tenure,* is to be published by NeWest Press in Sept. 2021.

In a former life he published around twenty more or less academic books, with forty or so translations into about twenty other languages.

For further information on Kieran visit Wikipedia
https://en.wikipedia.org/wiki/Kieran_Egan_(philosopher)

I have known the silence of the stars and of the sea,
And the silence of the city when it pauses . . .

~ Edgar Lee Masters